S0-AQK-736

**To be Rich
One Needs Millions!**

**The
Golden Rule
Club** ᴿ
**of
THE UNITED STATES
and
CANADA**

*To be Wealthy
You Need good
health, good friends
and a few
Bucks!*

International Headquarters:

**9000 Sunset Blvd.
Hollywood, Ca. 90069
213+274-4900**

I'm Patty Thomas -- I've performed for you
many times on the Bob Hope shows.

To keep busy doing something worthwhile,
I've accepted the offer to become
Secretary of The Golden Rule Club.

You must be a very fine person and
a very solid citizen. Why? Because a
<u>good friend of yours</u> has sent us a check
to buy a wonderful Gift for you.

A wonderful new book is being mailed you
today direct by THE KAYBEE PRESS, INC.
The Donor, your friend's name, will be
inside.

Your good friend <u>also bought you</u>
Jimmy Clark's Musical Review of this
unique book. I will mail it to you -- but
first you need let me know if you have
a cassette player or record player.
I will mail you either a cassette or
the two records.

Please check which you wish and return
the enclosed post card today.

Sincerely yours,

Patty Thomas

Patty Thomas
for THE GOLDEN RULE CLUB

PT:b

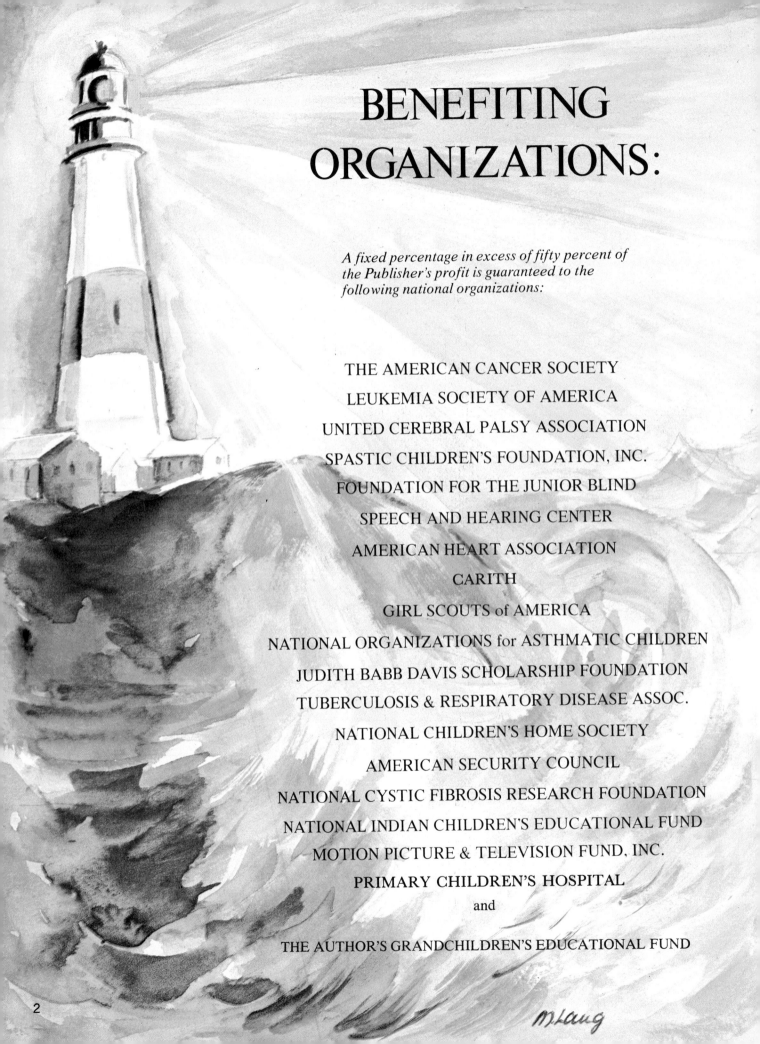

BENEFITING ORGANIZATIONS:

A fixed percentage in excess of fifty percent of the Publisher's profit is guaranteed to the following national organizations:

THE AMERICAN CANCER SOCIETY

LEUKEMIA SOCIETY OF AMERICA

UNITED CEREBRAL PALSY ASSOCIATION

SPASTIC CHILDREN'S FOUNDATION, INC.

FOUNDATION FOR THE JUNIOR BLIND

SPEECH AND HEARING CENTER

AMERICAN HEART ASSOCIATION

CARITH

GIRL SCOUTS of AMERICA

NATIONAL ORGANIZATIONS for ASTHMATIC CHILDREN

JUDITH BABB DAVIS SCHOLARSHIP FOUNDATION

TUBERCULOSIS & RESPIRATORY DISEASE ASSOC.

NATIONAL CHILDREN'S HOME SOCIETY

AMERICAN SECURITY COUNCIL

NATIONAL CYSTIC FIBROSIS RESEARCH FOUNDATION

NATIONAL INDIAN CHILDREN'S EDUCATIONAL FUND

MOTION PICTURE & TELEVISION FUND, INC.

PRIMARY CHILDREN'S HOSPITAL

and

THE AUTHOR'S GRANDCHILDREN'S EDUCATIONAL FUND

2

m.Lang

CHILDREN...

Our Most Precious Possession!

WE WHO ARE
HEALTHY MUST
ALWAYS BE WILLING
TO HELP THOSE WHO
ARE NOT.

—ILA HUNT CRANE

4

POEMS ABOUT GOD

Ila Hunt Crane

Paintings by Marie Lang

COPYRIGHT   U.S.A., 1972
(All Rights Reserved)

by

H. KROGER BABB
Publisher

Library of Congress Catalog Card Number:
71-162851; ISBN 0-87786-002-5

Published by THE KAYBEE PRESS, 9000 Sunset Blvd.,
Hollywood, Calif., U.S.A., 90069. *Printed in
the U.S.A. *All Foreign Rights reserved. *Foreign Language
Rights owned and reserved by Harold Straubing,
Summit Publishing Company.

FIRST PRINTING—250,000 COPIES

(Reproduction in whole or part forbidden by any person or media without written permission.)

Ila Hunt Crane

(1918—1971)

".. I dedicate these poems to my children, Tamara, Martha and Thomas and my grandchildren.."
—ILA HUNT CRANE

Born Aug. 14th, 1918, in Richfield, a small town in the heart of the beautiful state of Utah, Ila Hunt was educated and grew to womanhood there. Our author was surrounded by 2 brothers, 4 sisters, her parents and a town full of God-loving neighbors.

Never anticipating fame as an author, her goal in life was to guide and teach youngsters how to find happiness and understand God.

Although a good wife and busy mother, Ila found time and love for everyone's children. She enthused youngsters, taught them to swim, cook and appreciate the great outdoors. Her lessons in creative stitchery thrilled every girl.

"POEMS ABOUT GOD" for all Faiths in all States were written by Ila Hunt Crane in a Southern California Hospital, shortly before her death, Jan. 11, 1971.

"GOD BLESS THIS UNUSUAL BOOK..."

Calvin L. Rampton
GOVERNOR
UTAH

William A. Egan
GOVERNOR
ALASKA

Stanley K. Hathaway
GOVERNOR
WYOMING

George C. Wallace
GOVERNOR
ALABAMA

William G. Miliken
GOVERNOR
MICHIGAN

Richard B. Ogilvie
GOVERNOR
ILLINOIS

Tom McCall
GOVERNOR
OREGON

Milton J. Shapp
GOVERNOR
PENNSYLVANIA

John J. McKeithen
GOVERNOR
LOUISIANA

Jimmy Carter
GOVERNOR
GEORGIA

Winfield Dunn
GOVERNOR
TENNESSEE

Richard S. Kneip
GOVERNOR
SOUTH DAKOTA

Bruce King
GOVERNOR
NEW MEXICO

Reubin Askew
GOVERNOR
FLORIDA

Frank Licht
GOVERNOR
RHODE ISLAND

James Exon
GOVERNOR
NEBRASKA

Jack Williams
GOVERNOR
ARIZONA

Russell W. Peterson
GOVERNOR
DELAWARE

William L. Guy
GOVERNOR
NORTH DAKOTA

11

13

CHILDREN of ALABAMA

God has many houses,
Scattered far and wide.
And in each one of them you'll find
God living there inside.

For our bodies are like houses,
And God is living there,
So we must always treat our house,
With deep respect and care.

Now what you do to others,
You do to yourself too
For God is part of everyone,
Just as He's part of you.

M. Lang

CHILDREN of ALASKA

My little one . . . oh do you know . . .
That while you rest . . . God helps you grow?

I know a game that you can play . . .
But you must do each thing I say.

Lie very straight and very still . . .
Then wriggle your toes as hard as you will.

Now make them quiet and jiggle your knees . . .
Like leaves when the wind blows through the trees.

Now move your hips around and around
In sort of a circle, without a sound.

Now drum your fingers, if you will,
Like the pecking of birds . . . on a window sill.

Now it's time to feel your breathing go
In and out . . . . deep . . . and slow.

Next wriggle your jaw . . . . then crinkle your nose . . .
Then roll your eyes . . . . and let each lid close.

Now let your mind . . . as it leaves your face . . .
Slip deep inside . . . to the quiet place . . .

Where only you and God can go . . . .
And as you rest . . . . God helps you grow.

CHILDREN of ARIZONA

Please show me, God, the way to go,
Show me the way, so I will know
All of the things that I should do,
In ways that you would want me to.

I'd like to be of use to You.
Please show me, God, what I should do,
Where I should go, what I should be . . .
The things that You have planned for me.

But while I'm waiting day by day,
For you to come and show the way,
I'll do the very best I know
So I'll be ready, God, to go.

CHILDREN of ARKANSAS

Dear God . . . . .

If I can teach a child to pray . . .
Or help another on his way . . .
If I can be of use to you . . . . .
This is all I want to do.

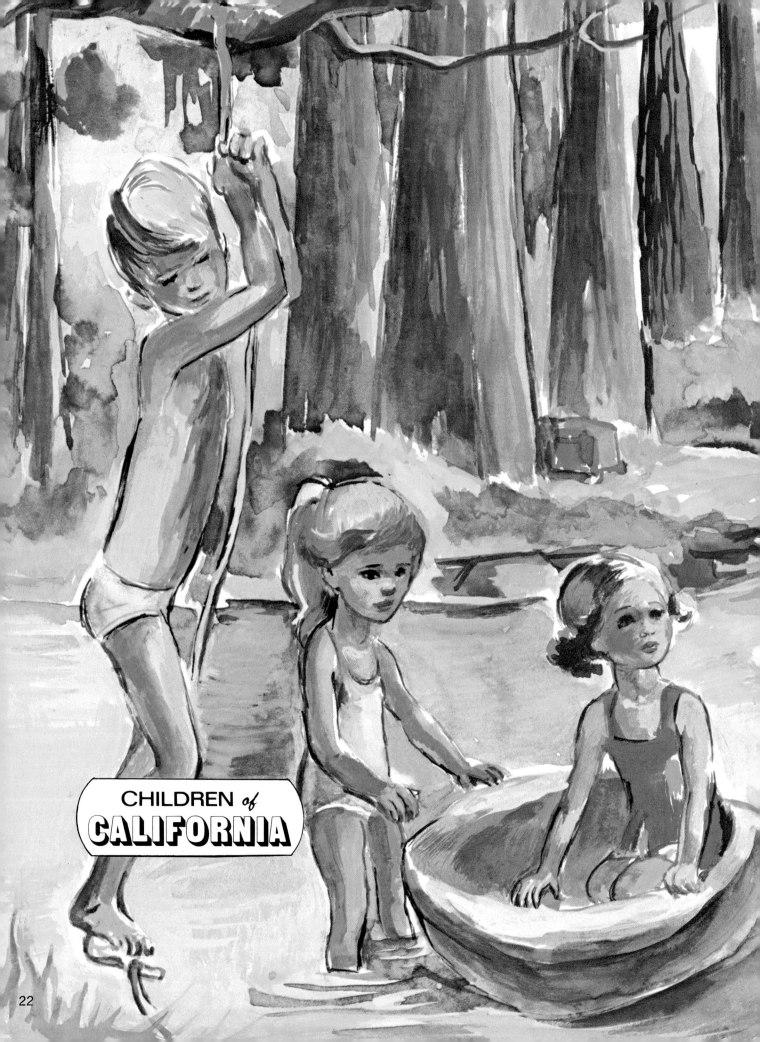

CHILDREN of
CALIFORNIA

Good food and sleep will make me grow,
And I will do the best I know . . .
So I will grow both straight and tall,
And will not always stay this small.

And there is something else I know.
Good thoughts and deeds make spirits grow.
I'll strive to be in every way . . . .
Better today . . . than yesterday.

My spirit self must not stay small . . .
While my body self is growing tall.
I want my inner self, you see . . . .
Growing big . . . along with me.

mlang

CHILDREN of COLORADO

Good Morning, God, I pray to you,
To bless this day, while it is new.

God, bless me too, that I might be,
So very, very near to Thee.

And in your presence, safe and warm,
To be protected from all harm.

Please guide me so that I might do,
All of the things you want me to.

And when the sun has finally set,
There'll be no sorrow or regret.

For I have done the best I could,
And I have done the things I should.

And when it ends, then I can say,
Thanks, God, for giving me this day.

mlang

CHILDREN of
CONNECTICUT

God is merciful and kind,
And I relax in His loving care.
In everything I say or do,
I know that God is there.

CHILDREN of
DELAWARE

Baby, playing in the sand,
You come from a Holy Land
All alone, and all unknown
To become my very own.

Though I know you can't recall
The joys of that fair place at all,
His Goodness I can plainly see
Who sent you here to be with me.

M. Lang

CHILDREN of FLORIDA

30

There are days when you feel lonely,
Days when there's nothing much to do.
Even Mother is too busy
To come and play with you.

There is a game that you can play,
It's called, "God's Good To Me".
And you can count what God has done
In everything you do or see.

You sit, you stand, you walk around,
With no one else to tell or show.
For you must find these things yourself,
With only you and God to know.

You think, you count, you look about,
Then how happy you will be.
Soon you'll be glad you had the time,
To play the game, "God's Good To Me".

M. Lang

CHILDREN of GEORGIA

God, I know there are things that I must do.
I know there are things I should trust to You.

Forgiveness and faith in Your ways are mine.
Justice and judgement of others are Thine.

God, please help me to see my own part through,
And then to leave all the rest, God, up to You.

CHILDREN of HAWAII

If trouble should happen to come my way,
Give me the courage to bear it.
Send me a smile, along with the tears,
Then teach me, Oh God, how to wear it.

CHILDREN of IDAHO

Oh, please, God, help me to be good.
To think and say the things I should.
Sometimes it's very hard for me
To be the things I ought to be.

And though I know you're always near,
Sometimes I do not want to hear.
And when you show the way to me,
Then I pretend I cannot see.

God, in your wise and loving way,
Please teach me what to do and say.
Please help my heart to always know
The way that you would have me go.

And help me so that I may find
A way to always be more kind.
Help me to do the things I should.
Oh, please, God, help me to be good.

MLang

CHILDREN of ILLINOIS

Like a plane that flies above a storm
You rise from trouble into a warm
Knowledge of His love so dear
It banishes your every fear.
A moment ago the storm was nigh,
You struggled beneath a leaden sky,
But now the sun is shining bright
For you've been guided by His light.

CHILDREN of INDIANA

When someone says, "God Bless You."
But does nothing much about it.
I don't think that God can hear,
However loud they shout it.

But when you do a kindly deed,
For one that is distressed,
And do it very quietly,
It's then that God hears best.

M. Lang

While you are busy in your play,
With games or toys throughout the day,
Sometimes it's hard to understand
How dirt collects upon your hands.

Then Mother says, "It's a disgrace!
Now go wash your hands and face!"
Sometimes you have to change your clothes,
Though where dirt comes from . . . goodness knows!

Now you should know that through the day,
When someone's anger comes your way . . .
And makes you have some hateful thoughts.
These also leave some dirty spots.

Though these are hidden deep within,
Yet you must wash away the sin.
Forgive yourself and others too.
God's love will make you clean and new.

Go find a little quiet place . . .
Then trade bad thoughts for love and grace.
Love and forgiveness makes one whole . . .
Like soap and water for the soul.

CHILDREN of KANSAS

God wants you with Him all week long
Through thoughts, through deeds, through bits of song.
To show him that you are aware
Of His holy spirit always there.

If you forget him through the week . . .
And then on Sunday try to seek
His love, His joy, His peace of mind . . .
I think perhaps you're going to find . . .

The house of God a little bare . . .
You cannot feel His spirit there.
So be with Him the whole week through . . .
Then Sunday . . . God can be with you.

CHILDREN of KENTUCKY

Now God is here and God is there.
You know that God is everywhere.

But do you know the thrilling part?
That God is living in your heart?

He speaks through you, He acts through you,
So mind each little thing you do.

Yes, speak and act with utmost care,
And make God glad He's living there.

CHILDREN of LOUISIANA

In prayer and praise,
I come to Thee,
To thank You for
Your love for me.

My heart is filled
With a glad glow,
Because, dear God,
You love me so.

For all the goodness
Shown to me,
In prayer and praise,
I come to Thee.

49

CHILDREN of MAINE

God wants you well, God wants you strong,
God wants you happy all day long.

But did you know that it takes two?
That it takes God . . . . but also you?

Because . . . before the blessings start . . .
First . . . you must open up your heart.

The secret here . . . is that one must
Have a key called Faith and Trust.

And when your heart is opened wide . . . .
Then God can place His gifts inside.

CHILDREN of MARYLAND

I like to sit upon a hill,
Where things are far away and still.

Away up high where I can see
For miles and miles in front of me.

Oh it is such a pleasant place
With the sun so warm upon my face,

And it's so quiet I can hear
The grasses whisper in my ear.

And though my body feels quite small . . . .
Inside of me keeps growing tall.

The earth, the sky, the golden sun,
And God and I . . . . . all feel like one.

M. Lang

CHILDREN of
MASSACHUSETTS

God, with you some part of me is safe in store,
And while it is, I know of fear no more.
The things that trouble me soon pass away
As long as from Your path I never stray.
Whatever is Your will, I am resigned
No greater wisdom will I ever find,
And it will always put my soul at rest
To know that what You planned for me is best.

CHILDREN of MICHIGAN

Sometimes when I do something bad,
I feel so mean and small.
And though I say I do not care . . .
I don't feel good at all.

But when I do my very best . . .
To do the things I should.
I feel so warm, so proud and tall . . .
Just knowing I've been good.

I think that God . . . inside of me . . .
Gives me that happy glow . . .
And makes me glad . . . and makes me smile . . .
And that is why I know . . . .

That I don't need to win a prize . . .
To put up on the shelf.
It's just that I like being good . . . .
Because I please myself.

CHILDREN of
MINNESOTA

God . . . touch my soul . . . that it may grow . . .
Then teach my heart . . . to always know . . .
Through faith, through love, through simple grace . .
We have a sacred meeting place.

A place where you and I can speak . . .
When I feel troubled . . . small . . . and weak.
And find the answers . . . know you care.
Then . . . thank you . . . God . . . for being there.

M. Lang

Before you go to the Land of Nod . . .
Lie quietly . . . and think of God.

Lie quietly and think of Him . . .
And know that God lies deep within.

Yes, deep within your heart and mind
Just waiting there for you to find.

How vast His loving, tender care.
And know that He is always there.

Now send your thoughts and prayers of love . . .
But send them to His home above.

To thank Him for His tender care . . .
For God, you know, is everywhere.

Before you go to the Land of Nod . . . .
Lie quietly . . . . and think of God.

mLang

61

CHILDREN of MISSOURI

Today someone accused me
Of things I didn't do.
And when I said I didn't . . .
They said it was untrue.

At first it made me feel so sad . . .
It even made me cry.
Then I remembered that God knew . . .
I hadn't told a lie.

And then my heart felt happy . . .
And I thought of it no more.
It is for God in Heaven
To know my thoughts are pure.

It's for me . . . to be forgiving . . .
And learn to hold no grudge.
It is for God to know the truth . . .
For God to be the judge.

M. Lang

CHILDREN of MONTANA

Just trust in God . . . in all you do.
And know . . . that He will see you through.

In every problem . . . . you will find . . .
That trust in God . . . will ease your mind.

Just trust in God . . . when things go wrong.
You'll find you still can sing a song.

There'll be no need for tears or fear.
Just trust in God . . . He's always near.

To have a peaceful path to trod . . .
With every step . . . just trust in God.

CHILDREN of NEBRASKA

How many kinds of animals . . . .
How many kinds of birds we see . . .
If we just look then we would know . . .
God loves to have variety.

So many kinds of flowers . . .
Each one a different hue.
And when God made His children . . .
He made them different too.

His love for one is just as much . . .
As it is for the others . . .
If we would think . . . then we would know . . .
That all of us are brothers.

CHILDREN of NEVADA

After I have said my prayers . . . .
I stop . . . and listen . . . quietly.
Because I think that God should have . . .
A chance . . . to also . . . talk to me.

CHILDREN of
NEW HAMPSHIRE

When Mother's busy all the day,
And there's no friend with which to play,
No one to tell my secrets to,
I know that I can talk to You.

When there's a cold within my head,
And Mother makes me stay in bed,
There's nothing much that I can do,
I'm grateful I can talk to You.

And on those days when all I see
Are people being cross with me,
I know You love me, this is true,
For I can always talk to You.

Thank you, God, for being near,
For being close, where You can hear.
When I am troubled, sad, or blue,
It makes me glad . . . to talk to You.

M. Lang

CHILDREN of
NEW JERSEY

On the way to school this morning
With your face all sleepy, yawning
Suddenly stopped for a tree in bloom.
You'll learn much more than in any classroom
About our world, and how it was made
By God's own sunshine in God's own shade.

M. Lang

CHILDREN of
NEW MEXICO

You are God's child, but also mine . . . .
A body with a soul divine.
He placed you in my loving hands . . . .
To help you learn and understand.

To help you grow in every way . . . .
In truth . . . . in stature . . . every day.
To keep you pure and undefiled . . .
To help you know . . . you are God's child.

God trusted me to train you right . . .
For you are holy in his sight.
So I must teach you how to pray . . .
And how to act and to obey.

To teach you rules of honesty . . .
For God has trusted you to me.
We will not question how or why . . .
You are God's child . . . and so am I.

CHILDREN of NEW YORK

When walking on a city street
Watch the faces that you meet
Some are sad, and some wear frowns
As if their little ups and downs
Had made them permanently sad,
And there's no comfort to be had.
Yet we know that there's someone near
Who gives our hearts eternal cheer
So when our moment's trouble is through
We find God walking with us, too.

M. Lang

Each day is like
A precious stone,
That God has let
Me call my own.

As to its worth?
What shall it be?
Well, God has left
That up to me.

CHILDREN of
NORTH DAKOTA

Snowflakes, white and pure and soft,
Fall from angels high aloft.
I feel them touch my nose and hair
And then I know that everywhere
I am watching God's great hand
Pour His whiteness on our land.

CHILDREN of OHIO

When you are grateful . .
You're richer by far . . .
Than anyone might
Ever think that you are.

And when you are down
On your bended knee
You are taller then
Than you'll ever be.

83

CHILDREN of OKLAHOMA

I know there are things that I must do.
I know there are things to trust to You.

Forgiveness and faith in Your ways are mine.
And justice, and judging of others are Thine.

Help me to see my own part through,
And leave the rest, God, up to You.

Sometimes . . . . when I used to pray . . .
I'd think of God . . . as far away.
I'd think of Him as way up high . . . .
Living somewhere in the sky.

But now I know He's always near . . .
And that's the reason he can hear
Every thought and word I say . . . .
Even when I do not pray.

If I should do what isn't right . . .
I cannot keep it from His sight.
I cannot run away and hide . . .
For God is living deep inside.

CHILDREN of
PENNSYLVANIA

God, who greens the land in Spring
Also gives us songs to sing
Hymns of joy to fields a-greening
Baby new birds chirping, preening.

These are ways that God does take
To show the wonders He can make
His goodness and His mighty power
Shown alike in song and shower.

CHILDREN of
RHODE ISLAND

Was this a day when things went wrong?
You feel as though you don't belong?

Did someone treat you mean or cruel,
Forgetting there's a Golden Rule?

Don't fret or worry, have no fear . . . .
Because, you see, God loves you, dear.

Was this a day you were not good?
And did not do the things you should?

With anger in your heart and mind . . . .
Were you the one to be unkind?

A fresh new day will soon be here,
And all the time — God loves you, dear.

CHILDREN of
SOUTH CAROLINA

His spirit far more gently passes
Than dew on morning's summer grasses,
Than music whose notes softly fall
Within a silent cloistered hall.
A spirit that on your soul does lie
Closer than eyelid on an eye.
It tells you of a sweeter calm,
And can be found in slumber's balm.
The peace that from God's heaven does go
To bless us in this world below.

M. Lang

93

Thank You, God, in every way.
Thanks for giving me this day.
For my life and for my health,
For the earth and all its wealth.

For everyone that I hold dear,
For knowing, God, that You are near.
I'm grateful for the knowledge, too,
That all good things have come from You.

There's a time to work,
There's a time to play.
A time to eat,
A time to pray.

There's a time to sleep,
And a time to dare.
But all the time
Dear — God is there.

To guard you in sleep,
To guide you in play.
To bless the food
You eat each day.

For God watches you
With His loving care.
Yes, all the time
Dear . . . God is there.

CHILDREN of TEXAS

Open my eyes that I might see
Truth and its reality.

Open my ears that I might hear
Your voice and know that You are near.

Touch my heart that I might know
Love and compassion as I go.

Direct my life that I might trod
The path that leads to You, oh God.

M Lang

CHILDREN of UTAH

Sometimes when you do something nice . . .
And someone thanks you . . . maybe twice . . . .

To know that they appreciate . . .
Just makes you feel so good . . . so great . . .

It even makes you feel quite sure . . .
You'd like to do a little more.

Now . . . think what God has done for you . . .
I think He'd like some "Thank You's" too.

M. Lang

CHILDREN of VERMONT

Dress up as neatly as you can
Everything just spick-and-span.
Sunday is a special day
It's when we all must go to pray
And reverently spend an hour
Worshipping Him who made the flower
In His house we'll sing a hymn
That lift our voices up to Him.

CHILDREN *of* VIRGINIA

Oh little one, oh do you know . . .
What makes the pretty flowers grow?

What bursts their seeds, then breaks through earth . . .
Into a miracle of birth?

Oh little one, oh do you know . . .
What is it then that makes you grow?

What makes you breathe? How beats your heart?
And who has fashioned every part?

I do not have to tell you so . . .
Because I think, somehow, you know.

M. Lang

CHILDREN of WASHINGTON

They say that daisies never tell.
But I can hear them very well.
With leaves outspread — with hearts laid bare —
They speak of God's true loving care.

In words of sweet simplicity . . .
They speak of God's great love for me.
That's how I know that daisies tell . . .
In fact — I hear them very well.

M. Lang

Oh pretty deer with so much grace
You each have such a happy face.
You are so brave and do not cry
When men shoot just to see you die.

Much happiness is what you give
All God's children want you to live.
But even if your life is brief
Our Love for you relieves our grief.

At night when I am in my bed,
My mother comes to stroke my head
To kiss me, and while bending low,
She whispers, "Dear, I love you so."

And all night long I think I hear
Her soft voice whisper in my ear.
It makes me glad, for though I know,
I like it when she tells me so.

It makes me feel so very good,
I want to do the things I should.
God, I'm so very glad you see
That's she's the one you chose for me.

CHILDREN of WYOMING

Good night, God, and as I sleep,
Your tender, loving care will keep
Me safe from harm all through the night.
For I am precious in Thy sight.

I sleep so calm and peacefully,
Knowing of your love for me.
When I awake, I shall thank You,
By being kind and loving too.

The United States of America,
a government of the people,
by the people, for the people.

PROTECT YOUR COUNTRY, STATE AND HOME TOWN. SUPPORT YOUR LOCAL POLICE. VOTE.

DLang

A MOTHER'S LOVE—

The Most Powerful
Force in The World.

Ila Hunt Crane

116

118

A HAPPY LIFE IS A
COMBINATION OF
MAKING THE RIGHT
DECISIONS. WHEN IT'S
THE LAST INNING, THE
BASES ARE LOADED
AND TWO ARE OUT — A
GROWING BOY NEEDS
TO DECIDE IF HE
WOULD RATHER BE
THE PITCHER OR THE
BATTER.

—ILA HUNT
(Quote from a high school
essay, Richfield, Utah, 1934)

119

A YOUNGSTER'S
FIRST TRIP TO A
ZOO, IS LIKE A
GIRL'S FIRST KISS
IN A CANOE—
NEVER FORGOTTEN.

—ILA HUNT CRANE.

121

SWIMMING is such clean, wonderful exercise and fun.

—ILA HUNT CRANE

123

Our Young Art Director Bob Marble chose Marie Lang to do the original water colors for this book.

MARIE LANG is a native of Boston, Mass., a graduate of Brookline Hi and Boston's famous Museum School of Fine Arts.

WHILE SHE was teaching art in the Ithaca, N.Y. high school, Marie continued her studies at Cornell.

MOTHER OF 3 children, today Marie lives with her husband, dog and cat in the Pacific Palisades, where her studio is but a stone's throw from the rolling blue Pacific.

INDEX:

WITH BEAUTIFUL 3-dimensional frames, or without, Lithograph full-color reproductions (11″ x 17″) of all paintings and poems are available for your children's bedrooms.
—THE KAYBEE PRESS, INC.

CREDITS:

Author: *Ila Hunt Crane*
Art Director: *Bob Marble*
Artist: *Marie Lang*
Format & Design:
  Kroger Babb
Supervision:
  Harold Straubing
Authorization:
  Ila & Albert Crane
Legal: *Judge Charles R. Kirk,*
  Attorney Ezra Stern,
  Attorney Irving Fields

Research: *TIF*
  West: *Rena Knee*
  Northwest: *Mary Helmhout*
  Northcentral:
    Shirley Herreid
  Southwest: *Darlene Bridges*
  Midwest: *Roz Young*
  South: *Ginger Prince Hall*
  Eastern Seaboard:
    Martha Duke
  East: *Linda Sherman*
  New England:
    Irene McNally

Editor: *Mildred Horn Babb*
Photography: *Stu Stallsmith*
Director Printing:
  Herbert Aronson.

World-wide English language Editions: **THE KAYBEE PRESS**, 9000 Sunset Blvd., Hollywood, Calif. 90069.

Publication date:
  Aug. 14th, 1972

World-wide Foreign language Editions: The Summit Publishing Co., Canoga Park, California 91306.